Houghton Mifflin Harcourt
Biology

Indiana Academic Standards for
Science Guide

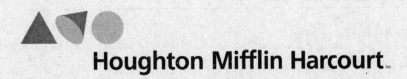

ISBN 978-1-328-77340-1

2 3 4 5 6 7 8 9 10   0982   25 24 23 22 21 20 19 18 17

4500655052   A B C D E F G

Contents

Indiana Academic Standards for Science Guide

Introduction

This guide provides activities to help you prepare for the Indiana Academic Standards for Science. For each standard, you will find a Challenge Activity that is posed as a performance task—a lab or an investigation, a research project, or another activity. The task addresses the standard or a significant part of it.

Indiana Academic Standards for Science

Cellular Structure and Function

B.1.1   Compare and contrast the shape and function of the essential biological macro-molecules (i.e. carbohydrates, lipids, proteins, and nucleic acids), as well as, how chemical elements (i.e. carbon, hydrogen, oxygen, nitrogen, phosphorus, and sulfur) can combine to form these biomolecules.

B.1.2   Analyze how the shape of a molecule determines its role in the many different types of cellular processes (e.g., metabolism, homeostasis, growth and development, and heredity) and understand that the majority of these processes involve proteins that act as enzymes.

B.1.3   Develop and use models that illustrate how a cell membrane regulates the uptake of materials essential for growth and survival while removing or preventing harmful waste materials from accumulating through the processes of active and passive transport.

B.1.4   Develop and use models to illustrate how specialized structures within cells (i.e. nuclei, ribosomes, Golgi, endoplasmic reticulum) interact to produce, modify, and transport proteins.

B.1.5   Develop and use a model to illustrate the hierarchical organization of interacting systems (cell, tissue, organ, organ system) that provide specific functions within multicellular organisms.

Matter Cycles and Energy Transfer

B.2.1   Use a model to illustrate how photosynthesis transforms light energy into stored chemical energy.

B.2.2   Use a model to illustrate that cellular respiration is a chemical process whereby the bonds of food molecules and oxygen molecules are broken and the bonds in new compounds are formed resulting in a net transfer of energy.

B.2.3   Use mathematical and/or computational representations to support claims for the cycling of matter and flow of energy among organisms in an ecosystem.

B.2.4   Develop a model to illustrate the role of photosynthesis and cellular respiration in the cycling of carbon among the biosphere, atmosphere, hydrosphere, and geo-sphere.

Interdependence

B.3.1   Use mathematical and/or computational representation to explain why the carrying capacity ecosystems can support is limited by the available energy, water, oxygen, and minerals and by the ability of ecosystems to recycle the remains of dead organisms.

B.3.2   Design, evaluate, and refine a model which shows how human activities and natural phenomena can change the flow of matter and energy in an ecosystem and how those changes impact the environment and biodiversity of populations in ecosystems of different scales, as well as, how these human impacts can be reduced.

B.3.3   Evaluate the claims, evidence, and reasoning that the complex interactions in ecosystems maintain relatively consistent numbers and types of organisms in stable conditions, and identify the impact of changing conditions or introducing non-native species into that ecosystem.

Indiana Academic Standards for Science

Inheritance and Variation of Traits

B.4.1 Develop and revise a model that clarifies the relationship between DNA and chromosomes in coding the instructions for characteristic traits passed from parents to offspring.

B.4.2 Construct an explanation for how the structure of DNA determines the structure of proteins which carry out the essential functions of life through systems of specialized cells.

B.4.3 Construct a model to explain that the unique shape and function of each protein is determined by the sequence of its amino acids, and thus is determined by the sequence of the DNA that codes for this protein.

B.4.4 Use a model to illustrate the role of cellular division (mitosis) and differentiation in producing and maintaining complex organisms.

B.4.5 Make and defend a claim based on evidence that inheritable genetic variations may result from: (1) new genetic combinations through meiosis, (2) viable errors occurring during replication, and (3) mutations caused by environmental factors.

B.4.6 Apply concepts of statistics and probability to explain the variation and distribution of expressed traits in a population.

Evolution

B.5.1 Evaluate anatomical and molecular evidence to provide an explanation of how organisms are classified and named based on their evolutionary relationships into taxonomic categories.

B.5.2 Communicate scientific information that common ancestry and biological evolution are supported by multiple lines of empirical evidence including both anatomical and molecular evidence.

B.5.3 Apply concepts of statistics and probability to support a claim that organisms with an advantageous heritable trait tend to increase in proportion to organisms lacking this trait.

B.5.4 Evaluate evidence to explain the role of natural selection as an evolutionary mechanism that leads to the adaptation of species, and to support claims that changes in environmental conditions may result in: (1) increases in the number of individuals of some species, (2) the emergence of new species over time, and/or (3) the extinction of other species.

B.5.5 Construct an explanation based on evidence that the process of evolution primarily results from four factors: (1) the potential for a species to increase in number, (2) the heritable genetic variation of individuals in a species due to mutation and sexual reproduction, (3) competition for limited resources, and (4) the proliferation of those organisms that are better able to survive and reproduce in the environment.

B.5.6 Analyze and interpret data for patterns in the fossil record and molecular data that document the existence, diversity, extinction, and change of life forms throughout the history of life on Earth under the assumption that natural laws operate today as in the past.

Cellular Structure and Function

B.1.1: Molecules of Life

B.1.1 Compare and contrast the shape and function of the essential biological macromolecules (i.e. carbohydrates, lipids, proteins, and nucleic acids), as well as, how chemical elements (i.e. carbon, hydrogen, oxygen, nitrogen, phosphorus, and sulfur) can combine to form these biomolecules.

Challenge Activity

Challenge: Gather evidence and create a poster explaining how elements from sugar molecules combine with other elements to form the carbon-based molecules needed for life.

Living things are made up of different types of organic, or carbon-based, molecules. When we eat food, our digestive system breaks the food into smaller molecules that can be used by the body. Once digestion is complete, nutrients are absorbed by the body and transported by the circulatory system and lymphatic system to all the cells.

Once food molecules enter cells, they can be broken down further to harness energy and form new types of molecules. For example, sugar molecules contain the elements necessary to produce many other types of organic molecules. These elements can be rearranged and combined with other elements through chemical reactions to form new products, such as proteins, fats, and DNA.

In this Challenge Activity, you will make a poster for your school cafeteria that will help your fellow students understand the molecules in their bodies and in the foods they eat. Your poster should explain what organic molecules are composed of, how they are made, and how they function in the human body.

MATERIALS

- Chapter 2 Virtual Investigation: Macromolecules of Life
- computer with Internet access
- markers or colored pencils
- poster paper, butcher paper, or large construction paper

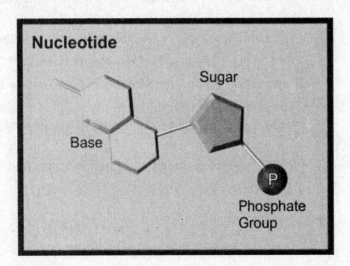

MEET THE CHALLENGE

1. Review the Documentation section.

2. Complete the Chapter 2 Virtual Investigation: Macromolecules of Life. The Virtual Investigation is in the Interactive section of the Student Resources that accompanies the *Student Edition.* As you complete the virtual investigation, write notes or draw diagrams that will help you construct your poster.

3. Use your notes to create a poster. If you need more evidence, you can use additional sources. Make sure you use reliable sources, such as educational institutions, government agencies, and peer-reviewed articles.

4. Cite your sources on your poster or on a separate sheet of paper. Follow the format provided by your teacher.

DOCUMENTATION

1. Create a poster explaining how elements from sugar molecules combine with other elements to form the carbon-based molecules needed for life. Your poster should contain text and/or diagrams that address each of the following sections.

2. **Organic Molecules** Include the following in your description of organic molecules:
   - What are organic molecules?
   - Why are organic molecules important for living things?
   - How do living things obtain organic molecules?

3. **Composition of Organic Molecules** Explain the following for each type of organic molecule—carbohydrate, lipid, protein, and nucleic acid:
   - What is this biomolecule made up of? Discuss the subunits and the elements within the subunits. Include diagrams if necessary.
   - What are some functions of this biomolecule in the cell or body?
   - What types of food is this biomolecule found in?

4. **Construction of Organic Molecules** Explain how macromolecules are made.
   - The elements in sugar molecules are used to construct other types of organic molecules. What elements do sugars have in common with every other type of organic molecule?
   - How do enzymes aid in the formation of macromolecules?

B.1.2: Structure and Function of Molecules

B.1.2 Analyze how the shape of a molecule determines its role in the many different types of cellular processes (e.g., metabolism, homeostasis, growth and development, and heredity) and understand that the majority of these processes involve proteins that act as enzymes.

Challenge Activity

Challenge: Gather evidence and create a poster that shows how the molecular shape of an enzyme determines its role in a cellular process.

Enzymes are large molecules, or macromolecules, that catalyze a biochemical reaction. Enzymes have very specific shapes that other molecules, called substrates, can attach to or "fit." The enzyme interacts with another molecule or substrate and converts it into new products, which are then released from the enzyme. For example, in the transcription of DNA, a segment of DNA is copied into RNA (mRNA) by the enzyme RNA polymerase. The shape of this enzyme is part of the reason why it can pick up the nucleotides needed to build the strand of mRNA. The breakdown of hydrogen peroxide (H_2O_2) in the bodies of many animals is another example. H_2O_2 is poisonous to many organisms but is enzymatically destroyed before it does any harm. H_2O_2 is broken down to oxygen and water. Even though this chemical reaction occurs spontaneously, the enzyme catalase increases the breakdown rate of the H_2O_2 substrate. In this Challenge Activity, you will make a poster for your class that will help fellow students understand why the shape of an enzyme molecule is very important in carrying out its function as a catalyst in a biochemical reaction. Your poster should show a model of an enzyme and its substrate and the different stages the enzyme would go through when catalyzing the reaction. This would include explaining the three steps: binding, conformational change in the enzyme (induced fit), and release. The poster should also show how the substrate has changed once released from the enzyme macromolecule.

MATERIALS

- computer with Internet access
- markers or colored pencils
- online resources: Step 2 in "Meeting the Challenge"
- poster paper, butcher paper, or large construction paper

MEET THE CHALLENGE

1. Review the Documentation section.

2. Complete reviewing the resources: Enzymes (Section 2.5); Enzymatic Activity (Section 2.5); Modeling Transcription (Section 8.4); Vernier Probeware Lab: Enzyme Action: Testing Catalase Activity (Section 2.5).

3. Use your notes to create a poster. If you need more evidence, you can use additional sources. Make sure you use reliable sources such as educational institutions, government agencies, and peer-reviewed articles.

4. Cite your sources on your poster or on a separate sheet of paper. Follow the format provided by your teacher.

PLANNING QUESTIONS

1. What is the structure and function of an enzyme?

2. What is a substrate?

3. Why do enzymes and substrates "fit" together?

4. What steps do the enzyme and substrate go through when they interact?

DOCUMENTATION

Create a poster that shows how the molecular shape of an enzyme determines its role in a cellular process such as the transcription of DNA. Your poster should contain text and/or diagrams that address each of the following sections.

- Structure and function of enzymes. Include the following in your description:
  - What are protein macromolecules made up of?
  - Are protein macromolecules enzymes?
  - Why are enzymes called catalysts?
- Interaction of enzymes with substrate. Include the following in your description:
  - Why do enzymes not interact with all substrates?
  - Describe what takes place during initial binding.
  - Explain what is meant by an "induced fit."
  - How is the substrate released once the reaction occurs?
- Products of enzyme-substrate interaction. Include the following in your description:
  - How is the substrate different after the interaction with the enzyme catalyst?
  - Does the chemical structure of the enzyme change once the chemical reaction is complete?
  - Do the effects of an induced fit remain on the enzyme's molecular structure?

Cellular Structure and Function

B.1.3: Feedback Mechanisms and Homeostasis

B.1.3 Develop and use models that illustrate how a cell membrane regulates the uptake of materials essential for growth and survival while removing or preventing harmful waste materials from accumulating through the processes of active and passive transport.

Challenge Activity

Challenge: Investigate one of the control systems that maintain homeostasis in the human body. Design and carry out an experiment to test understanding of a negative feedback loop in that system. Make hypotheses about how cell membranes in the body regulate homeostasis in the process that you have chosen.

BACKGROUND

Even if you've never heard of negative feedback loops and control systems, you use them all the time. Feedback loops let you know when to eat and drink, when you need a nap, and when you should turn on a fan to cool off. Altogether, the many feedback loops within your control systems help your body maintain homeostasis. It can be complicated to explain negative feedback loops in words. A flow chart can simplify the process by showing the important information in a few symbols.

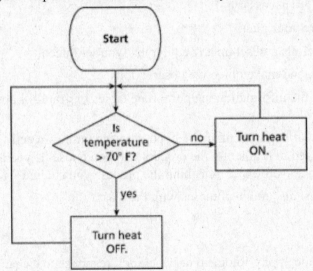

In each negative feedback loop in the body, there is a cell membrane that regulates the flow of materials. For example, when our body temperature increases, the cell membranes in the sweat ducts in the skin allow water to flow into the duct, thus increasing the amount of sweat produced. When we cool off, the cell membranes do not allow water to collect in the ducts, thus we stop sweating. In this lab, you'll create a flow chart for one of the control systems that keeps your body in homeostasis. You could study the control system that regulates your blood pressure or the oxygen and carbon dioxide content of your blood. Based on the flow chart, you can generate hypotheses.

The next step is to develop and conduct an experiment to test your hypothesis. Based on the results, you can revise your hypothesis and/or your experiment's design. Finally, you will generate hypotheses about how cell membranes help to regulate this process.

SAFETY

• Observe all safety precautions that are appropriate for your experiment.

MEET THE CHALLENGE

1. Choose a control system in the human body that maintains homeostasis through negative feedback loops. Some possibilities include temperature, blood levels of oxygen and carbon dioxide, blood pressure, and blood sugar. Be sure that the control system you choose can be tested in a classroom setting.

2. Prepare a flow chart that shows one or two negative feedback loops of your control system. Use separate flow charts as necessary for additional feedback loops.

3. Use your flow chart to generate one or more testable hypotheses.

4. Develop a classroom experiment that will test one of your hypotheses by using your classmates as subjects. Consider safety, cost, time limitations, and the availability of materials in your experiment's design. You may develop a survey to test your hypothesis if a hands-on test is not realistic. Consult with your teacher as needed.

5. Write out a procedure plan for your experiment. Make the following decisions:
   • how you will test your hypothesis
   • what materials and technology you will need
   • what the experimental control(s) will be
   • what safety procedures are necessary

6. Have your teacher approve your plan.

7. Obtain the necessary materials and set up any equipment you will need.

8. Conduct your experiment, and make objective observations.

9. Collect data and organize the information in appropriate tables or graphs. Label the graphs and tables properly.

10. After you have finished your experiment, make hypotheses about how a cell membrane could be involved in regulating the process that you chose. If you are not sure where to begin, try to do some research about the process you studied.

11. Share your results, conclusions, and hypotheses with the class.

TIP

• Your hypothesis should predict a physiological or behavioral response to a change in the body's internal environment.

DOCUMENTATION

1. **Summarize Data** Summarize your findings and observations, including an analysis of your data tables or graphs.

2. **Evaluate** Did your results support your hypothesis? Explain why or why not.

3. **Synthesize** Provide evidence from your experiment and your research that feedback mechanisms and cell membranes maintain homeostasis. Include test results from your final experiment.

B.1.4: Cell Diversity

B.1.4 Develop and use models to illustrate how specialized structures within cells (i.e. nuclei, ribosomes, Golgi, endoplasmic reticulum) interact to produce, modify, and transport proteins.

Challenge Activity

Challenge: Obtain information from valid sources and make a children's book that provides an overview of cellular structure and function in plant and animal cells.

Plant and animal cells have some chemical, structural, and functional features in common, but they also contain structures unique to their specific functions. Each cell is like a small-scale factory, with different organelles (structures) performing jobs that contribute to the overall function of the cell. Because plant and animal cells have different roles, some of their organelles are the same and some are different.

In this Challenge Activity, you will make a children's book that will help other students understand the role of specialized structures within animal and plant cells. Your book should explain the functions of each of the organelles in the cell and how their organelle's structure is related to its function. Your book should specifically highlight information about which structures are involved in the production, modification, and transport of proteins in the cell.

MATERIALS

- computer with Internet access
- markers or colored pencils
- presentation binder or stapler

MEET THE CHALLENGE

1. Review the Documentation section as you prepare to research different cell structures.

2. Research and take notes on plant and animal cells. Take notes on what structures are found in each type of cell and detail the structure's function. Pay special attention to any structure that is involved in the production or modification of proteins. Make sure to document your sources.

3. For information not provided by your textbook, use additional resources. Make sure to use reliable sources such as websites from government agencies and educational institutions.

4. Use your notes to make a children's book. Keep your intended audience in mind as you make your book so that it is engaging and at an appropriate level for their comprehension.

5. Use footnotes to document your sources on the pages of your book or in the endnotes. Follow the format provided by your teacher.

TIPS

• Compare and describe the cell structure and the organelles found in plant cells and animal cells. As you are identifying the functions of certain structures, try to make connections between different cell structures based on their job in the cell. (For example, how does the job of the ribosome relate to the job of the endoplasmic reticulum?)

• Keep in mind how the different cell structures and the variety of organelles found in plant and animal cells are related to the cell's function.

• Make illustrations neat and colorful, so they are easy to read, and add interest to your book.

DOCUMENTATION

1. **Apply** How are some of the organelles in the cell connected to each other based on their function? What would happen if one of these structures was missing from the cell?

2. **Analyze** How are the cell diagrams helpful? How are they misleading?

3. **Synthesize** Bacterial cells are prokaryotic, and plant and animal cells are eukaryotic. Fungal cells have multiple nuclei. Do you think they are prokaryotic or eukaryotic? Explain.

B.1.5: Interacting Systems

B.1.5 Develop and use a model to illustrate the hierarchical organization of interacting systems (cell, tissue, organ, organ system) that provide specific functions within multicellular organisms.

Challenge Activity

Challenge: Study a plant's root, stem, and leaves to develop a model that illustrates how water and nutrients flow through the plant.

Roots, stems, and leaves are important plant organs. Roots anchor a plant to the ground and absorb water and minerals that the plant needs to grow. Fibrous root systems make fine branches in which most of the roots are the same size. These roots spread like a mat beneath the soil surface and firmly anchor the plant to the ground. Taproot systems have a long, thick, vertical root with smaller branches. Long taproots allow plants to get water from deep in the ground.

Stems provide support and house the vascular systems of the plant. Some stems are herbaceous. Herbaceous plants produce little or no wood. Stems can also be woody. A tree trunk is an example of a woody stem. Tissues in stems transport materials throughout the plant and can provide storage for food or water.

The leaves of plants are the main sites for photosynthesis, the essential process by which plants obtain and store energy.

Plants have many shapes, sizes, and adaptations to live in a variety of environments. The structural characteristics of specific roots, stems, and leaves relate to the plants' overall function in plant growth, development, and survival in their environment.

MATERIALS

- compound microscope
- cover slips (3)
- eyedropper
- model materials (will vary)
- plant root, stem, and leaf
- razor tool
- slides (3)
- water

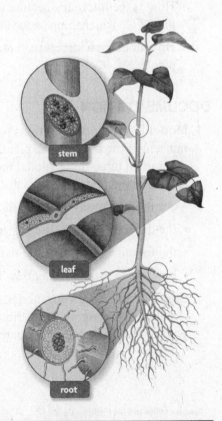

SAFETY

Use caution when using the razor blades. Always cut away from any part of your body and wash your hands after completing the lab.

MEET THE CHALLENGE

1. Choose a plant from the selection provided by your teacher.

2. Do research to learn about the environment in which the plant lives.

3. Make observations of the physical structures of the plant.

4. Organize your observations to help you plan and develop your model.

5. Carefully use the razor tool to cut a very thin slice from the root, stem, and leaf of the plant. You must be able to see light through the sliced sections.

6. Prepare a wet mount slide of a slice of each plant organ. Examine each slide under the microscope.

7. Make observations of the internal structures of the plant organs.

8. Organize your observations to help you plan and develop your model.

TIP

When making observations and planning for your model, consider the following questions:

- How are the structures of the plant related to specific functions in growth and survival? How does the environment influence the structure of the plant?

- What similarities did you observe among the slides of the three plant organs? Explain why these similarities may exist.

- Which organ had the most vessels? Which organ had the most chloroplasts? Which organ had the most hairs? Is this what you would predict based on the function of these organs?

- How is the internal structure of the plant related to the external structure of the plant? Consider things such as plant height, root depth, and leaf size and thickness.

- How does each structure contribute to the flow of water and nutrients through the plant?

DOCUMENTATION

1. **Model** Use your observations to develop a model that illustrates how water and nutrients flow through the plant. Your model may be in the form of a flipbook, a diagram, a three-dimensional model, a computer graphic, or another format. Your teacher should approve your format before you begin.

   Your model should illustrate the following information:

   - the different plant tissue systems
   - the function of each of the tissue systems
   - how water and nutrients flow through the plant

2. **Summarize** Using your model, summarize your observations. For each plant structure you observed, describe how it might contribute to the plant's survival. Share your results with your classmates to compare models and observations.

B.2.1: Photosynthesis

B.2.1 Use a model to illustrate how photosynthesis transforms light energy into stored chemical energy.

Challenge Activity

Challenge: In this activity you will test the effect of different light sources on the rate of photosynthesis and illustrate your findings.

Photosynthesis converts some of the energy absorbed from sunlight into the chemical energy of sugars. The process is also the major source of oxygen in Earth's atmosphere. By measuring oxygen production indirectly, you can measure the rate of photosynthesis. Remember that a rate describes how one quantity changes compared with another. In this lab you will design an experiment to determine the effect of different light sources on the rate of photosynthesis in leaves.

MATERIALS

- beaker, 100 mL
- forceps
- hole punch
- ivy leaves, young
- light source, strong
- $NaHCO_3$/detergent solution
- stopwatch
- syringe, plastic, 10 cc
- water

SAFETY

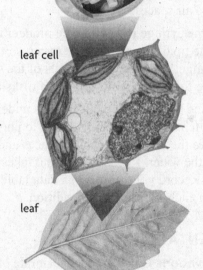

chloroplast

leaf cell

leaf

MEET THE CHALLENGE

1. Decide how to test different light sources on the rate of photosynthesis. Identify your independent variable. Have your teacher approve your choice.

2. Identify your control condition and the constants in the experiment. Examples of constants are the temperature of the water and the distance between the light and the beaker.

3. Write the procedure for your experiment. Test the rate of photosynthesis using your procedure.

4. Use the hole punch to make five disks from an ivy leaf.

B.2.1: Photosynthesis *continued*

5. Fill one beaker halfway with the sodium bicarbonate/detergent solution. Fill a second beaker with water.

6. Remove the plunger from the syringe and place the ivy leaf disks into the syringe. Insert the plunger and draw 5 cc (5 mL) of the sodium bicarbonate/detergent solution into the syringe as shown.

7. Hold the syringe so that the tip is pointing upward. Push on the plunger to squirt out any air in the syringe. Place your finger on the tip of the syringe as shown. Withdraw the plunger to form a vacuum, but be careful not to pull the plunger all the way out of the syringe. When the vacuum is formed, the gases in the air spaces of the leaf disks move into the syringe and the solution diffuses into the air spaces. Shake the syringe several times while your finger is on the tip.

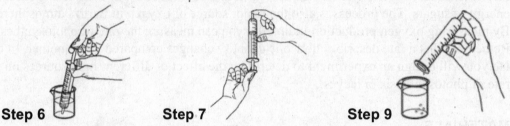

Step 6   **Step 7**   **Step 9**

8. Take your finger off of the tip of the syringe. This causes the leaf disks to sink to the bottom of the syringe because they become more dense from the diffusion of solution into the air spaces.

9. Open the syringe by pulling the plunger almost all the way out. Place your finger over the tip of the syringe and turn it so the tip is pointing down. Carefully remove the plunger and pour the contents of the syringe into the beaker of water as shown. Use the forceps to remove the leaf disks if they stick to the walls of the syringe.

10. Place the beaker with the leaf disks under the light source and immediately start the stopwatch. As the leaf disks begin to photosynthesize, the production of oxygen replaces the solution in the air spaces and the disks become less dense and float to the top of the water. Record the time it takes for each leaf disk to float to the top of the water. Record your results in a data table. Continue collecting data until all five disks float in each experimental condition.

DOCUMENTATION

1. **Observations** Calculate the mean rate of photosynthesis in each condition of your experiment using the formula:

$$\frac{5 \text{ (\# disks floating)}}{\text{total time (s)}} = \underline{\hspace{2cm}} \text{disks/s}$$

Determine the best type of graph to use to represent your data. Explain your choice and construct the graph. Be sure to carefully label the axes of the graph.

2. **Relate** How does this lab model photosynthesis? Using the model as a guideline, draw an illustration of photosynthesis in a leaf. Do the following in your illustration:

   • Label and trace the inputs and outputs of reactants and products.

   • Identify the transfer and/or transformation of energy.

3. **Extend** How does this lab setup compare to the way photosynthesis occurs in plants and other photosynthesizing organisms?

Matter Cycles and Energy Transfer

B.2.2: Cellular Respiration

B.2.2 Use a model to illustrate that cellular respiration is a chemical process whereby the bonds of food molecules and oxygen molecules are broken and the bonds in new compounds are formed resulting in a net transfer of energy.

Challenge Activity

Challenge: Investigate cellular respiration in dormant and germinated seeds to understand how germinating seeds obtain energy for germination and growth.

Germination occurs when a dormant seed begins to sprout and grow into a seedling. The following are some of the steps in the germination process:

- The seed coat softens and allows for absorption of water.
- The seed swells and the coat cracks and opens, allowing oxygen to become available to cells.
- Enzymes break down starch stored within the seed into glucose molecules that move in the cells.

MATERIALS

- beaker, 100 mL
- cotton plugs (6)
- KOH powder, 1.5 tsp
- marking pen
- rubber band
- ruler, metric
- seeds, dry (6)
- seeds, presoaked (6)
- test tubes (3)
- water, colored, 25 mL

SAFETY

Potassium hydroxide (KOH) is a strong base; avoid contact with eyes, skin, and clothing.

MEET THE CHALLENGE

1. Label the three test tubes: Tube 1: presoaked seeds; Tube 2: dry seeds; Tube 3: no seeds.

2. Layer into the test tubes the following materials. Make sure the layers are compact but not too tight:

   • Tube 1: presoaked seeds, cotton plug, $\frac{1}{2}$ tsp potassium hydroxide, cotton plug

   • Tube 2: dry seeds, cotton plug, $\frac{1}{2}$ tsp potassium hydroxide, cotton plug

   • Tube 3: cotton plug, $\frac{1}{2}$ tsp potassium hydroxide, cotton plug

3. Use the rubber band to hold the three test tubes together.

4. Invert the test tubes and place them in the beaker as shown. Wait 15 minutes.

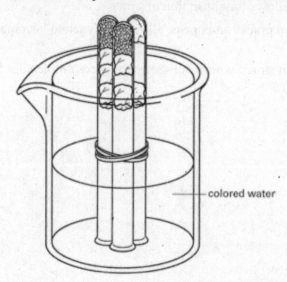

5. Measure the distance (in centimeters) that the colored water travels up each of the three test tubes. Record your results in a table.

6. Choose the type of graph that best represents the data. Construct your graph.

DOCUMENTATION

1. **Observations** Describe your observations and measurements of Tubes 1 and 2. What do the data show? Explain why differences between the two tubes might exist.

2. **Relate** How does this lab setup model cellular respiration? Using the model as a guideline, draw an illustration of cellular respiration in a germinating seed. Do the following in your illustration:

   • Label and trace the inputs and outputs of reactants and products.

   • Identify the transfer and/or transformation of energy.

   • Include the germination steps described at the beginning of this Challenge Activity.

3. **Extend** How does this lab setup compare with the way cellular respiration occurs in plants, animals, and other eukaryotes?

B.2.3: Pyramid Models

B.2.3 Use mathematical and/or computational representations to support claims for the cycling of matter and flow of energy among organisms in an ecosystem.

Challenge Activity

Challenge: Use pyramid models to represent the cycling of matter and flow of energy among organisms in an ecosystem.

MODELING ENERGY AND MATTER FLOW IN ECOSYSTEMS

Sunlight is the primary source of energy for most ecosystems. Producers, such as shrubs, use the energy from sunlight to make food. Herbivores, such as rabbits, eat the shrubs. Carnivores, such as foxes, eat the herbivores. However, not all of the energy from one trophic level reaches the trophic level above it. Some of the energy is used by the animal to grow. The remaining energy may be used to help fuel metabolic processes, such as cellular respiration, or remain undigested. In general, the loss of energy between trophic levels may be as high as 90%. This means that only 10% of the available energy is transferred from one trophic level to the next.

An *energy pyramid* is a diagram that compares the energy used by producers, primary consumers, and other trophic levels. The pyramid illustrates how available energy is distributed among trophic levels in an ecosystem. A biomass pyramid and a pyramid of numbers are two other types of pyramid models. A *biomass pyramid* is a diagram that compares the biomass of different trophic levels within an ecosystem. A *pyramid of numbers* shows the numbers of individual organisms at each trophic level in an ecosystem.

MATERIALS

- beaker, 1000 mL
- plastic cups, small and clear (3)
- water

energy
lost

energy transferred

B.2.3: Pyramid Models *continued*

MEET THE CHALLENGE

1. Add 1000 mL of water to the beaker. The beaker full of water represents the first trophic level in an energy pyramid.

2. Recall that 90% of the energy is lost to the environment as heat between trophic levels. Calculate how much water should be poured into the first cup to represent the transfer of energy from the first trophic level to the second.

3. How much energy is transferred from the second trophic level to the third trophic level? Calculate how much water should be poured into the second cup.

4. Finally, how much energy is transferred from the third trophic level to the fourth trophic level? Calculate how much water should be poured into the third cup.

DOCUMENTATION

1. **Illustrate** Draw an energy pyramid that illustrates the amount of energy you calculated for each trophic level in the Challenge Activity. Include the labels "producers," "primary consumers," "secondary consumers," and "tertiary consumers" on your illustration.

2. **Model** An energy pyramid illustrates the flow of energy through an ecosystem. How could you model the cycling of matter through the same ecosystem? Develop a model that would show the cycling of matter in an ecosystem. Your model may use the same, additional, or different materials than the items used in the energy pyramid activity.

3. **Extend** Choose an ecosystem. Draw a sample energy pyramid that might represent energy within that ecosystem. Include the names of different species that would be found at each trophic level. Then, using your knowledge of matter cycles, explain how a molecule of oxygen would cycle through the ecosystem.

B.2.4: The Carbon Cycle

B.2.4 Develop a model to illustrate the role of photosynthesis and cellular respiration in the cycling of carbon among the biosphere, atmosphere, hydrosphere, and geosphere.

Challenge Activity

Challenge: Study the transfer of carbon through snails and *Elodea* and then develop a model to illustrate the carbon cycle.

BACKGROUND

Carbon dioxide is a reactant in photosynthesis and a product of cellular respiration. Plants take in carbon dioxide from the atmosphere and use it as a source of carbon for the sugars they produce, such as glucose ($C_6H_{12}O_6$). Sunlight captured by the plant during photosynthesis is stored as chemical potential energy within the glucose molecules made by the plant. The overall process of photosynthesis is summarized as:

$$6CO_2 + 6H_2O + \text{light energy} \rightarrow C_6H_{12}O_6 + 6O_2$$

All organisms use food molecules, like glucose, to produce adenosine triphosphate (ATP). Made during cellular respiration, ATP provides cells with the energy needed for cell activities. Plants and other autotrophs make their own food; heterotrophs consume other organisms as food. To release the stored energy contained within the food molecules, an organism carries out respiration. The overall process of cellular respiration is summarized as:

$$C_6H_{12}O_6 + 6O_2 \rightarrow 6CO_2 + 6H_2O + ATP$$

Photosynthesis and cellular respiration are important components of the carbon cycle. As a result of these processes, carbon is exchanged between living things and the nonliving environment.

MATERIALS

- aquatic snails (2)
- bromothymol blue solution in dropper bottles
- *Elodea* sprigs (4)
- grow light
- labeling tape
- marker
- pH probe or pH paper
- test tube rack
- test tubes with stoppers, large (4)
- water, dechlorinated, 500 mL

SAFETY

MEET THE CHALLENGE

1. Label four test tubes "1," "2," "3," and "4."

2. Fill each test tube about three-quarters full with water.

3. Add ten drops of the bromothymol blue solution to each of the four test tubes.

4. Add one snail to Tube #2. Note: You will add nothing to Tube #1. Why?

5. Add two sprigs of *Elodea* to Tube #3.

6. Add two sprigs of *Elodea* and one snail to Tube #4.

7. Measure the pH of each test tube and record the initial pH values.

8. Seal all of the tubes so no air can enter or escape.

9. Place the test tubes near a light source for at least 24 hours. Make sure that the tubes will not get too hot during the incubation.

10. Predict how the pH may change in each of the tubes over the next 24 hours. Record your predictions.

11. Observe the color of the liquid in the test tubes after 24 hours, and record your observations.

12. Unseal the tubes, measure the pH of each, and record these final pH values.

13. Calculate the change in pH and record the values.
Change in pH = final pH – initial pH

14. Use your observations to develop a model to illustrate the carbon cycle.

TIP

When planning for your model, consider the following questions:

- What are the possible sources of carbon? Remember that carbon can be found in solid, liquid, and gaseous states.

- How is carbon transferred from the air, through living organisms, in the soil, and in water? How do the snails in the experiment affect the level of carbon dioxide in the water? How does *Elodea* affect the level of carbon dioxide in the water?

- Which test tube best illustrates a balanced system? Why?

DOCUMENTATION

1. **Develop a Model** Use your observations to develop a model to illustrate the carbon cycle.

2. **Format** Your model may be in the form of a diagram, 3D model, computer graphic or simulation, or other format. Your teacher should approve your format.

3. **Content** Your model should illustrate the following information:

   - how plants and animals play a role in the carbon cycle
   - the role of photosynthesis and cellular respiration in the carbon cycle
   - how carbon continually cycles through living organisms, a body of water, the atmosphere, and Earth's crust

4. **Extend** What would happen if the experiment were repeated in the dark?

B.3.1: Carrying Capacity

B.3.1 Use mathematical and/or computational representation to explain why the carrying capacity ecosystems can support is limited by the available energy, water, oxygen, and minerals and by the ability of ecosystems to recycle the remains of dead organisms.

Challenge Activity

Challenge: Model predation and the effects of changes in the environment on a population and the carrying capacity of the environment.

In this activity, your group will represent heron families that must catch fish to survive. In each generation, you will calculate the number of surviving individuals based on the amount of food collected. You will then graph the heron population over time to analyze the factors that affected your population.

Over time, the size of a population increases and decreases depending on factors including immigration, birth, emigration, and death. The growth of a population is a function of the environmental conditions. How fast a population grows is determined by the amount of resources available. There are two patterns of population growth. Exponential growth occurs when a population size increases dramatically over a period of time and is generally the result of abundant resources and low levels of predation. Logistic growth begins with a period of slow growth followed by rapid exponential growth before the population levels off at a carrying capacity. The carrying capacity of an environment is the maximum number of individuals of a particular species that the environment can normally and consistently support.

Population sizes are kept in check by limiting factors. A limiting factor is any environmental influence that directly affects a population size. Density-dependent limiting factors are those factors affected by the number of individuals living in a given area. They include competition, predation, and disease. Density-independent limiting factors are factors that limit the growth of a population regardless of its density. These factors include unusual weather, natural disasters, and human activities.

MATERIALS

For each group

- tray or paper, $21 \times 27 \text{ cm}^2$
- uncooked beans (50)

For each student

- paper cup

MEET THE CHALLENGE

1. Form groups of four students.

2. Place 50 "food units" (beans) on the tray.

3. For the first generation, you must collect two food units to survive. Taking turns, collect two food units at a time.

4. Record the number of surviving individuals in your data table. The number of surviving individuals for the first generation should be four.

5. Place all the food units back in the tray.

6. In the next generation, everybody in the group will have one offspring. To survive, you must collect two food units for yourself and two food units for each offspring.

7. Select a different group member to go first this time. Take turns collecting food, two units at a time, until everybody has enough food for themselves and their offspring. Record the number of surviving individuals for this generation (the second generation).

8. Repeat Steps 5–7 eight more times, recording the number of surviving individuals at each generation. The number of offspring that survive each generation depends on the amount of food that is gathered. For example, if your family consists of you and four offspring, but you only collect six food units, two of your offspring will die.

9. In the 11th generation, a drought causes the food units to decline. Place 30 food units in the tray instead of 50.

10. Repeat Steps 6 and 7 and record the number of surviving individuals.

11. In the 12th generation, the food stock is starting to recover. Place 40 food units in the tray.

12. Repeat Steps 6 and 7 and record the number of surviving individuals.

13. In the 13th generation, the food stock has completely recovered. Place 50 food units in the tray.

14. Repeat Steps 6 and 7 and record the number of surviving individuals.

15. In the 14th generation, predators are abundant. Each person loses two offspring to predators.

16. Repeat Steps 6 and 7 five more times and record the number of surviving individuals.

DOCUMENTATION

1. **Analyze** Graph and describe your data. Form conclusions about changes in the heron population. Include the following:

   • Create a graph of your data. Include a title and appropriate labels.

   • What is the carrying capacity of the ecosystem for the heron population?

   • What are the biotic and abiotic factors affecting the heron population?

   • How is food availability related to changes in biotic and abiotic factors?

   • Describe other biotic and abiotic factors that could affect the heron population.

2. **Using a Model** Identify and explain the limitations and constraints of your model.

B.3.2: Water Filter Design

B.3.2 Design, evaluate, and refine a model which shows how human activities and natural phenomena can change the flow of matter and energy in an ecosystem and how those changes impact the environment and biodiversity of populations in ecosystems of different scales, as well as, how these human impacts can be reduced.

Challenge Activity

Challenge: Design and conduct an experiment to determine what methods might be used to filter contaminants from a body of water.

ECOSYSTEM STABILITY AND KEYSTONE SPECIES

Runoff from a construction site is introducing sediment into Crescent Lake. The sediment is reaching the lake through a nearby stormwater pipe. Though once known as a premier wildlife viewing area, birdwatchers have noticed that fewer waterfowl species are now found on the lake, and state biologists have determined that amphibian and fish populations have also decreased drastically.

Water filtration is one process that can be used to remove materials from contaminated water. Natural substances, such as carbon, sand, clay soil, gravel, or rock, can be used to filter contaminants. These substances naturally filter impurities from Earth's surface water and groundwater. In this activity, you will design a filter for the stormwater pipe to prevent further sediment from entering Crescent Lake.

MATERIALS

Materials may include, but are not limited to:

- activated charcoal
- alum (potassium aluminum sulfate)
- aquarium gravel
- balance
- beakers (various sizes)
- brush (beaker or test tube)
- clay soil
- cotton balls and/or cotton gauze
- funnel (large)

- graduated cylinder, 100 mL
- gravel (coarse and fine separated)
- paper towels
- plastic bottle (1 L and 2 L)
- plastic cup (large)
- plastic spoon
- plastic tub or large plastic bowl
- sand (coarse and fine separated)
- water, contaminated (1 L)

SAFETY

- Always wear safety goggles, gloves, and a lab apron to protect your eyes and clothing.

- Do not touch any chemicals. If you get a chemical on your skin or clothing, wash the chemical off at the sink and alert your teacher.

- Alert your teacher in the event of a spill. Spills should be cleaned up promptly, according to your teacher's directions.

B.3.2: Water Filter Design *continued*

MEET THE CHALLENGE

1. **Create** Come up with a plan. Develop and conduct an experiment to determine what methods and materials can be used to best filter contaminants from a sample of water. Limit the number of conditions you choose for your experiment to those that can be completed during the time your teacher has allotted for this activity. Consult with your teacher to make sure that the conditions you have chosen are appropriate.

2. Write out a procedure for your experiment. Make the following decisions:
   - Decide what methods or materials you will test.
   - Decide how you will measure or determine whether a test is successful.
   - Select the materials and technology that you will need for your experiment from those that your teacher has provided.
   - Decide what your control(s) will be.
   - Decide what safety procedures are necessary.

3. Have your teacher approve your plans.

4. Obtain your materials and set up any apparatus you will need.

5. Take appropriate safety precautions.

6. Make objective observations.

7. Collect data and organize them into appropriate tables and/or graphs. Be certain that the graphs and tables are properly constructed and labeled. Compare the amounts and types of filtering materials used and determine which materials best filter the contaminated water sample.

8. Create a labeled diagram of your prototype, including any measurements.

9. Share your results with other teams. Elicit their feedback on your design.

10. Improve your design and test it.

DOCUMENTATION

1. Provide evidence of how your filter design addresses the challenge. Include test results from your final design.

2. **Features** Identify the main features of your design and the purpose of each. Include:
   - important components of the filtering device
   - a description of how the filtering device might have contributed to a decrease in contaminants in your water sample
   - a summary of your findings and observations, including an analysis of any data tables or graphs that you created

3. **Tradeoffs** Was your experiment a good model for showing what methods or materials might remove contaminants from water? Explain why or why not and give examples of what might be missing from your model.

4. **Conclusions** Describe how increased sedimentation in a lake could affect biodiversity. How might filtering the water change these effects? Is it possible to make the water too clean? Explain.

B.3.3: Ecosystem Stability

B.3.3 Evaluate the claims, evidence, and reasoning that the complex interactions in ecosystems maintain relatively consistent numbers and types of organisms in stable conditions, and identify the impact of changing conditions or introducing non-native species into that ecosystem.

Challenge Activity

Challenge: Use evidence and reasoning to explain how a disruption to ecosystem stability by the removal of a keystone species affects the numbers and types of organisms found there and why these changes may result in a new ecosystem.

ECOSYSTEM STABILITY AND KEYSTONE SPECIES

Because of the complex relationships found within an ecosystem, a single change can have a profound effect on the ecosystem as a whole. Some species have an unusually large impact on the ecosystem in which they live. These organisms are called *keystone species*. Examples of keystone species include sea otters in coastal marine ecosystems, wolves in boreal forest ecosystems, and prairie dogs in grassland ecosystems.

The removal of a keystone species from an ecosystem results in a cascade of changes that affect all of the remaining organisms within the ecosystem.

In this challenge, you will research a keystone species and use the evidence and reasoning provided in publications or other resources to evaluate the concept that the complex interactions in ecosystems maintain relatively consistent numbers and types of organisms in stable conditions, but changing conditions—for example, those resulting from the removal of a keystone species—may result in the formation of a new ecosystem. List the sources you use in a table like the one provided and then consider the questions that follow as you evaluate your sources and the evidence they provide.

MATERIALS

- Internet access
- news and information sources (for example, television newscasts, documentaries, expert interviews)
- reference books

MEET THE CHALLENGE

Use a table to organize your sources.

Source Title	Author(s)	Publication Year	Reliability (1 to 5)

QUESTIONS

• What criteria did you use to evaluate your sources? If the source contained data, how reliable do you think the data set is? Explain.

• How does your keystone species affect ecosystem stability? How might the ecosystem change if the keystone species is removed?

• After reviewing all your sources, what other studies do you think should be conducted to better understand the effects that keystone species have on ecosystem stability? Can a proven cause-and-effect relationship be established?

• Do you think that your sources are reliable? Can your sources all be equally trusted? What are some reasons why an author or group might wish to emphasize the effects of a keystone species? Why might other authors or groups wish to downplay them?

DOCUMENTATION

Prepare a poster, report, or other presentation describing the effects that your chosen keystone species has on ecosystem stability. Use your sources, as well as information from the *Student Edition*, to support your claims. As your teacher permits, the presentation can be completed on your own or in collaboration with others. If you can find a partner who has discovered other sources and formed an opinion that varies from your own, examine the differences among the sources and consider why your ideas might be different. In discussing your points, try to understand why some individuals or groups might hold a different opinion and directly address their concerns.

B.4.1: Investigating Albinism in Plants

B.4.1 Develop and revise a model that clarifies the relationship between DNA and chromosomes in coding the instructions for characteristic traits passed from parents to offspring.

Challenge Activity

Challenge: Formulate a question about albinism in tobacco plants, a model organism for plant genetic research. Design an experiment to investigate the question.

Although most tobacco plants have green leaves, there is a trait known as albinism that causes some tobacco plants to have white leaves. This trait is the result of an allele, or version of a gene, that can be passed from parent plants to their offspring. The seeds that you will use in this activity are the product of a cross between two green tobacco plants. However, you may observe the albinism trait in some of their offspring. Your challenge is to ask a question about the albinism allele in tobacco plants and design an experiment that will help you investigate your question.

MATERIALS
- filter paper
- light source
- paper, black
- petri dishes
- pipets
- tobacco seeds
- toothpicks
- water

SAFETY

Wear an apron to prevent chemicals or chemical solutions from contacting your skin or clothes. Safety goggles are required for performing this lab. Do not handle plants with your bare hands. Do not eat any part of a plant or plant seed used in the laboratory. Wash your hands thoroughly after handling any part of a plant. Dispose of contaminated materials, biological or chemical, in special containers, as directed by your teacher.

MEET THE CHALLENGE

1. With your partner or group, generate a question that you want to investigate about the albinism trait in tobacco plants. Your question can be related to whether the albinism allele is dominant or recessive, how the albinism trait affects growth, what proportion of plants will be albino, or how environmental factors affect the expression of the albinism trait. Have your teacher approve your question before continuing.

2. Write a hypothesis that predicts the outcome of your question.

3. Design an experiment to test your hypothesis. Write a procedure with numbered steps that includes an experimental variable, an experimental setup, a control setup, and constants. Have your teacher check your procedure before continuing.

4. Carry out your procedure. Begin by placing filter paper in petri dishes. Use a pipet to soak the filter paper with water.

5. Use a toothpick to spread the seeds evenly over the filter paper, and then place the covers on the dishes. Label the dishes according to the treatment they will receive.

6. Set up the remaining materials needed for your investigation, and track the growth of your seeds each day for one week. Record your data and observations in a table.

7. When your experiment is finished, complete the Documentation section.

8. Dispose of tobacco seeds as instructed by your teacher.

TIPS

- Environmental factors that could be investigated include the amount of light or water given to the plants.

- Data that could be collected include the number of plants of each color and the relative growth or health of the plants.

- Once you have determined what your experimental variable will be (the variable that you will change), design a control setup (a setup in which the variable is not changed).

DOCUMENTATION

1. **Analysis** Examine the data and draw conclusions. Consider the following questions:

   - How is it possible for two parent plants with green leaves to produce offspring with white leaves?

   - According to your results, is the albinism allele most likely dominant or recessive? How do you know?

   - For a cross in which both parent tobacco plants are green, 75% of the offspring are green and 25% of the offspring are albino. What are the genotypes of the parent plants? How do you know?

2. **Conclusion** State whether your data support your hypothesis.

   - Does the data you collected support your hypothesis?

   - Give specific evidence from your data and explain how it does or does not support your hypothesis.

   - Describe any sources of error that you think might have affected your data.

   - Explain how you would improve this investigation if you were to do it again.

B.4.2: Explaining Protein Synthesis

B.4.2 Construct an explanation for how the structure of DNA determines the structure of proteins which carry out the essential functions of life through systems of specialized cells.

Challenge Activity

Challenge: Create an informational guide explaining how the structure of DNA determines the structure of proteins and why it is important to understand these molecules.

The cell is the most basic unit of all living organisms. Contained within the cell's nucleus are molecules that carry the instructions for life. These molecules, known as DNA, serve as a template for making proteins. Proteins are chains of amino acids that carry out countless important jobs in the cell. Some of these jobs include catalyzing chemical reactions, transmitting information, providing structure, and transporting molecules throughout the cell.

DNA contains instructions for a large array of proteins, and these proteins are what allow cells to take on specialized roles. Specialized cells work together in multicellular organisms to perform all the functions needed for survival and reproduction. In this activity, your task is to create an informational guide that will help others understand the importance of these molecules and how they are constructed in the cell.

An informational guide conveys information in a brief and understandable way. Examples of such guides include pamphlets (small booklets), articles, videos, and public service announcements. As you begin gathering information about DNA and proteins, consider how you will summarize the information in an understandable way.

MATERIALS

- computer
- Internet access
- markers or colored pencils
- paper, various sizes

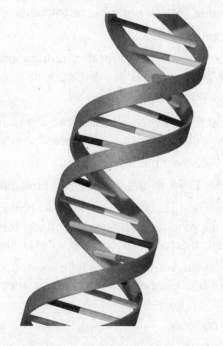

B.4.2: Explaining Protein Synthesis *continued*

MEET THE CHALLENGE

1. Use the Internet to search for information that will help answer the questions in the Planning section. Make sure to use information from credible sources, such as universities or government agencies. The webpage addresses for these sources often end with .edu or .gov. If you are not sure a source is credible, ask your teacher.

2. As you search, record your sources.

3. Use the guidelines in the Documentation section to create your informational guide.

PLANNING QUESTIONS

1. What is DNA?

2. Where in the cell is DNA located?

3. What is a gene?

4. What is a protein?

5. What are proteins made of?

6. How do proteins work in the body? Give some specific examples of protein types or functions and explain how they help specialized cells do their jobs.

7. How do cells use genes to make proteins?

8. What is transcription? Describe the basic steps of this process, where it occurs in the cell, and what the final product is.

9. What is translation? Describe the basic steps of this process, where it occurs in the cell, and what the final product is.

DOCUMENTATION

1. Use the Planning section and these instructions to create an informational guide.

2. **Audience** Choose the audience.

   • Decide who the audience is for this informational guide. The audience could include the general public or other students.

3. **Format** Choose a format.

   • Decide what format you will use to present your information, for example, a pamphlet, a website, a poster, a billboard, a video, or an article.

4. **Content** Include essential information.

   • Explain what DNA is, describe its structure, and tell where it is located in the cell.

   • Explain what genes are and describe how proteins are made from genes. Make sure to explain the processes of transcription and translation, including the basic steps in each process, where they occur, and what products are made.

   • Describe ways in which proteins help specialized cells carry out the essential functions of life. Give examples of protein functions in specialized cells.

B.4.3: Amino Acids and Proteins

B.4.3 Construct a model to explain that the unique shape and function of each protein is determined by the sequence of its amino acids, and thus is determined by the sequence of the DNA that codes for this protein.

Challenge Activity

Challenge: Create a modeling kit that teaches people to build the primary structure of specific proteins out of amino acid components and demonstrate how the amino acid order of the overall protein is just as critical to its shape as it is to its function.

Living things contain tens of thousands of different kinds of proteins. The human body can build approximately 100,000 different protein types, each with a highly specific structure and function. Proteins are not only used to build things like muscles, but also carry out diverse jobs in an organism, such as sending and receiving messages and moving materials around a cell. All enzymes are proteins that critically catalyze chemical reactions.

These protein types are all made from only 20 amino acids, similar to how all words in the English language are made from only 26 letters. Just as every word has its own meaning based on the order of the letters, each protein has its own function based on the order and arrangement of its amino acids. Amino acids link together into long chains, which then can bend and interconnect with others in many different shapes to build a final protein structure. The order of the amino acids is determined by the DNA genetic code. Any changes, errors, or mutations to the DNA or subsequent protein synthesis process can result in an inaccurate protein structure, which would affect the ability of the protein to carry out its function.

In this activity, you will create a modeling kit that allows people to build a primary structure protein out of amino acid components and learn about the other levels of protein structure. The kit gives people a way to learn about something through the use of physical materials to build objects or demonstrate processes. As you begin gathering information, consider what materials you may use for the modeling kit that would work for this activity.

MATERIALS

- computer
- Internet access
- printer to write and print out kit instructions, amino acid chart, examples of levels of protein structure, and other related information
- resealable bag or box to contain materials
- various materials for use as amino acids, which must be attachable, such as: paper clips, safety pins, paper and tape, interlocking building toy pieces, chemical modeling pieces, or other compatible materials

MEET THE CHALLENGE

1. Use the Internet to find specific proteins you would like to include in your kit, along with background information on them and their amino acid sequence. Develop or print out an amino acid chart that gives information about each acid, including its full name, abbreviated name, and overall charge.

2. As you search, record your sources.

3. Determine which materials you will include to represent and differentiate the amino acids and to show how they will be used to form the primary protein structure.

4. Use the guidelines in the Documentation section to create your modeling kit.

PLANNING QUESTIONS

1. What is an amino acid?

2. How many amino acids are there, and how do they differ?

3. What is a protein?

4. What is primary protein structure? Secondary? Tertiary? Quaternary?

5. What are proteins made of?

6. How do proteins work in the body? Give some specific examples of protein types or functions and explain how they help specialized cells do their jobs.

7. How does protein structure connect to the DNA code?

8. What can happen to a protein structure if there is an error in the amino acid sequence?

9. How does protein structure relate to inheritance?

DOCUMENTATION

1. Use the Planning section and these instructions to create a protein modeling kit.

2. **Audience** Choose the audience.

   • Decide who the audience is for this modeling kit guide. The audience could include the general public or other students.

3. **Format** Choose materials.

   • Decide what materials you will be using for your kit that can best represent amino acids and can be used to model a primary protein structure.

4. **Content** Include essential information.

   • Explain what amino acids are, and summarize how mRNA via DNA determines their sequence in a protein.

   • Explain the different types of protein structure, and how amino acid types affect it, especially in terms of electrical interactions.

   • Include specific proteins to model that are not too long, and provide background information on them. Show other types of protein structure beyond primary, but do not require users to model each of your protein examples.

B.4.4: Illustrating Cell Division and Differentiation

B.4.4 Use a model to illustrate the role of cellular division (mitosis) and differentiation in producing and maintaining complex organisms.

Challenge Activity

Challenge: Illustrate the role of cell division and differentiation in producing and maintaining multicellular organisms by creating a flipbook, comic strip, diagram, or flow chart.

Cellular division, or mitosis, is the process by which a cell divides into two cells. This process allows multicellular organisms to grow and repair their tissues. Cell differentiation is the process by which unspecialized cells develop specific forms and functions. Together, these processes create organisms that have specialized cells, tissues, and organs. These specialized structures work together to carry out complex functions, such as breathing, digesting, and pumping blood.

MATERIALS

- colored pencils or markers
- computers
- hole punch
- paper, various sizes
- scissors
- stapler
- string
- whiteboards, small

SAFETY

Exercise caution when using scissors and staplers.

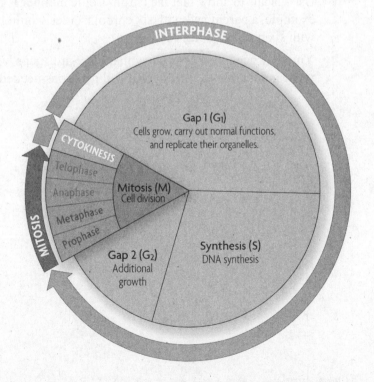

MEET THE CHALLENGE

Use the guidelines in the Documentation section and the diagram on the previous page to create your illustration.

PLANNING

1. **Section 5.5 Visual Concepts: Differentiation**

   What is differentiation? How does it produce a complex organism?

2. **Section 24.1 Visual Concepts: Tissue, Organ, and Organ System**

   How are cells organized in multicellular organisms?

DOCUMENTATION

1. Use your notes from the Planning section to create an illustration of the role of cell division and differentiation in producing and maintaining multicellular organisms.

2. **Format** Choose a format for your illustration.

   • Your illustration may be in the form of a flipbook, comic book, diagram, or flow chart. You may use an alternative format if your teacher approves.

   • Your illustration should show either the development of a multicellular organism or the process of cell repair.

   • Your illustration should be visual in nature and show uniqueness and creativity.

3. **Content** Include necessary information.

   • Include at least one visual for each step of the process. For the development of an organism, show fertilization, cell division (mitosis), and differentiation. For cell repair, show cell damage or loss, cell division (mitosis), and differentiation.

   • Use visuals to show that the chromosome number is conserved in cell division. For example, a parent cell with six chromosomes would produce two daughter cells with six chromosomes each.

   • You may need visuals to show that there are "gaps" in the illustration. For example, you cannot draw the millions of cell divisions needed to produce an organism.

B.4.5: Variation in Human Traits

B.4.5 Make and defend a claim based on evidence that inheritable genetic variations may result from: (1) new genetic combinations through meiosis, (2) viable errors occurring during replication, and (3) mutations caused by environmental factors.

Challenge Activity

Challenge: Gather evidence about processes that create genetic diversity and prepare for a roundtable discussion about the following question: Which has a greater effect on the diversity of human traits—nature or nurture?

The variety in human traits is vast. No two people are exactly the same in the way they look, act, and experience life. People have long wondered which has more influence on the variety that we observe in human traits—genetics or environment? This is sometimes referred to as the "nature versus nurture" debate.

   The differences we observe among humans are the result of genetic variation, or genetic diversity. Particular genes influence particular traits. Different variants of genes are called alleles. The more variation there is among alleles, the greater the genetic diversity. In this activity, you will gather evidence and make a claim about which has a greater effect on the genetic diversity of humans—our genetics or our environment.

MATERIALS

• computer, tablet, or personal device with Internet access

• *Student Edition*

DISCUSSION GUIDELINES

In this activity, you will participate in a roundtable discussion with your peers. Follow the guidelines below during the discussion.

• Arrange your desks so that everyone can participate. A circle or square works well.

• Raise your hand when you want to speak.

• Each person should speak at least once, but your teacher may require that you speak more than once.

• When speaking, acknowledge the speaker before you. For example, "I would like to add to what _____ said," "I agree with _____," or "I have a different opinion than _____ does."

• Always give evidence to support your claim. Provide the source and explain how the source supports your claim.

• Be polite when speaking and acknowledge other speakers. Do not use personal attacks.

MEET THE CHALLENGE

1. Use the Internet and/or Sections 6.6 and 8.7 of the *Student Edition* to find information that will help you answer the questions.

2. Write a claim using the guidelines in the Documentation section.

3. Use the Discussion Guidelines and participate in a roundtable discussion with your peers.

QUESTIONS

1. How does the independent assortment of chromosomes during meiosis create genetic diversity among an individual's gametes?

2. How does crossing over during meiosis create genetic diversity among an individual's gametes?

3. What is a mutation?

4. How do mutations arise during DNA replication?

5. How do factors in the environment cause mutations?

6. What are some examples of factors in the environment that can lead to mutations?

7. Are all mutations heritable? In other words, are they always passed down to the individual's offspring? Explain your answer.

8. Are all mutations expressed in an individual's phenotype? That is, do they always affect the physical makeup of the organism? Explain your answer.

9. If time allows, research a specific trait or disease that occurs in humans. Write a description of the trait or disease and explain how genetic and environmental factors affect its expression.

DOCUMENTATION

1. Prepare for a roundtable discussion by writing a claim about whether nature or nurture has a greater effect on human genetic diversity.

2. **Claim** Answer the following question:

   • In your opinion, which has a greater influence on the diversity of human traits— genetics (nature) or the environment (nurture)?

3. **Evidence** Outline the evidence to defend your claim.

   • List specific facts or statistics that you will use to defend your claim during the discussion. Include information about both meiosis and mutations.

   • List the sources of your facts or statistics. Include the title, author, source/publisher, and year published. Record specific page numbers if applicable.

4. **Reasoning** Connect the evidence to the claim.

   • Explain how the evidence you selected supports your claim.

5. **Discussion** Participate in a roundtable discussion with your peers.

   • Refer to the Discussion Guidelines provided before beginning the roundtable discussion.

B.4.6: Traits and Probability

B.4.6 Apply concepts of statistics and probability to explain the variation and distribution of expressed traits in a population.

Challenge Activity

Challenge: Model the distribution of alleles, calculate the probabilities of specific allele combinations, and apply your results to explain the variation of traits in a population.

Gregor Mendel mated thousands of pea plants and studied many traits among the offspring. For each experimental cross, he could easily observe whether subsequent generations produced peas that were wrinkled or smooth or if the plants were short or tall, but understanding why these traits appeared in some plants and not others was difficult.

Mendel did not know about alleles or meiosis when he began his observations, but he recognized patterns in the phenotypes generated by test crosses. In this Challenge Activity, you will model how alleles are distributed in a population and examine the probability of phenotypes.

Mendel's Experimental Cross

Traits that were hidden when parental purebred flowers were crossed reappeared when the F₁ generation was allowed to self-pollinate.

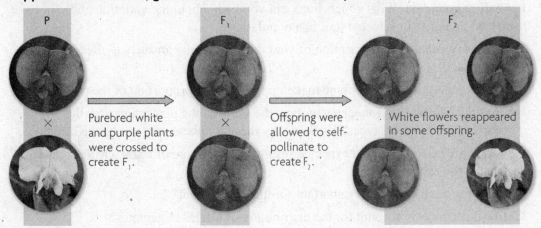

P   F₁   F₂

Purebred white and purple plants were crossed to create F₁.

Offspring were allowed to self-pollinate to create F₂.

White flowers reappeared in some offspring.

MATERIALS

• coins (2)

• marker

• tape, masking 4 cm

SAFETY

Be cautious when flipping coins so that they do not hurt you or your classmates.

MEET THE CHALLENGE

1. Using the coins, tape, and marker, label a set of two coins to simulate a monohybrid cross. Your teacher may recommend a particular cross for each group. Use a capital letter to represent a dominant allele (for example, *R* for round peas) and a lowercase letter to represent a recessive allele (for example, *r* for wrinkled peas). One coin should have the mother's gametes. The other coin should have the father's gametes.

2. Flip the two coins simultaneously. The two coins together make up the genetic material of the zygote. Record the genotype and phenotype of the offspring.

3. Repeat Step 2 for a total of 50 trials. Create a data table in which you can record the results of your coin tosses.

4. Calculate what percentage of offspring had each possible genotype and phenotype. Show your data and calculations to your teacher before moving on.

TIP

To calculate the percentage of offspring that had each possible genotype and phenotype, multiply by 2 the number of coin flips for each genotype or phenotype. Because you completed 50 trials, multiplying by 2 converts the number of coin flips to a portion of 100, or a percentage.

DOCUMENTATION

1. Analyze your data. What conclusions can you form about the variation and distribution of your selected trait in a population?

2. **Analyze** Write a brief description of your data, including answers to the following questions:

   • What genotype and phenotype make up the greatest proportion of the population?

   • Are the percentages for each genotype the same as the percentages for the corresponding phenotypes? Explain why these numbers may not be the same.

   • Compare your data to the expected results for your type of cross. Do your data match the expected data?

   • Was the number of trials important for this experiment?

3. How does meiosis account for the distribution of alleles to gametes?

4. Species that reproduce sexually (have gametes formed by meiosis) typically have greater variation in their populations than do species that reproduce asexually (have gametes formed by mitosis). Why might sexual reproduction lead to greater variation than asexual reproduction does?

5. **Conclude** Explain how the data you obtained apply to the variation and distribution of traits in a population.

B.5.1: Classification

B.5.1 Evaluate anatomical and molecular evidence to provide an explanation of how organisms are classified and named based on their evolutionary relationships into taxonomic categories.

Challenge Activity

Challenge: Students will obtain raw data on a set of organisms. Observing their physical characteristics, students will create a chart to compare similar and dissimilar traits. Based on their observations, students will generate hypotheses about how these organisms are grouped into taxonomic categories. Each group will present their conclusions to the class and explain the scientific process behind their classification.

BACKGROUND

In the early 1800s, Linnaeus created a system to organize and name the diversity of life. Prior to his work, organisms were referred to by their common name only. Imagine referring to very different creatures like tigers, lions, and domestic short hairs by the common name "cat." This was an inadequate system for scientists to communicate details. Linnaeus's method of binomial nomenclature helped to eliminate the confusion. Since then, scientists around the world can exchange information accurately because each organism now has a unique name.

Each group in taxonomy, or classification, is based on a series of levels. Organisms are organized into a large group first, called a kingdom, and then each kingdom is reorganized into subsequently smaller groups called phyla. Phyla are reorganized into classes, which are grouped into orders, then families until each organism is given a genus and species name. In this way, each level is restructured and organisms are grouped according to characteristics that reflect their similarity and evolutionary relationships.

All of the organisms that you will be selecting are grouped into the animal kingdom. Your task is to hypothesize a way that these animals can be classified into phyla, classes, and orders based on their similarities and differences.

MATERIALS

- computer access to presentation program
- paper to create charts

B.5.1: Classification *continued*

MEET THE CHALLENGE

1. Create a list of seven different organisms, one in each of the following categories:

    a. an invertebrate

    b. a fish

    c. an amphibian

    d. a reptile

    e. a bird

    f. a non-primate mammal

    g. a primate

2. Choose characteristics that you will use to evaluate your group of animals. Using your teacher's chart as a guide, create a chart of your characteristics and record data for each animal you have chosen.

3. Evaluate your collected observations for trends and similarities. As you begin to group your organisms, just like scientists today, start with the largest group(s). Which characteristics do most of them have in common? Does it make sense to group them together based on the characteristics you chose? Is there a better way to group them? Discuss in your group and arrive at a consensus. Once you have the largest group(s), or phylum, determined, look for characteristics that separate each phylum group further into smaller groups, or classes. Once you have your animals broken down into classes, break each class down into at least two smaller groups, called orders.

4. Label each individual with a genus and species name (you get to make these up; Linnaeus used Latin, but you can be creative!).

5. Make a computer presentation that thoroughly explains to the class how each of the animals were classified. The presentation must include the observations, the evaluation criteria for determining phylum, class, and order groups; and an explanation of the final taxonomic relationships. You should also provide an explanation of why you chose each animal's genus and species name.

TIPS

• The greater the number of characteristics used to evaluate your organisms, the more accurate your taxonomic conclusions. Try to choose at least 8 unique characteristics.

• Use pictures of the animals in your presentation to illustrate the observations used to determine groupings.

DOCUMENTATION

1. **Obtain Data** Using observable traits or characteristics, gather data on all animals.

2. **Evaluate** Using data gathered, determine taxonomic groupings.

3. **Communicate** Summarize observations using a classroom presentation that thoroughly addresses:

    • description of observations used to evaluate relationships between the animals

    • description of taxonomic relationships based on evaluation criteria

B.5.2: Communicating Evidence of Evolution

B.5.2 Communicate scientific information that common ancestry and biological evolution are supported by multiple lines of empirical evidence including both anatomical and molecular evidence.

Challenge Activity

Challenge: Examine several lines of evidence, including homologous structures, gene sequences, embryology, and fossil evidence, to determine how they support the theory of evolution, including the principles of change over time and common ancestry. Communicate findings in the form of a presentation or pamphlet.

Darwin spent many years collecting evidence of evolution from different fields. Since that time, technology has advanced, and the fields of genetics and molecular biology have added strong support to Darwin's theory of evolution by natural selection. In this activity, you will examine several lines of evidence, including homologous structures, gene sequences, embryology, and fossil evidence, to determine how they support the modern theory of evolution. You will then communicate your findings in the form of a presentation or pamphlet.

Homologous structures are organs or bones that appear in different animals but have apparent anatomical similarities. The human arm and whale flipper that appear in this activity are homologous structures. Molecular evidence for common ancestry includes DNA and protein sequences. DNA sequence analysis depends on the fact that the more related two organisms are, the more similar their DNA will be. The homeobox genes shown here are genes that control the development of specific structures. These sequences of genes are found in many organisms, from fruit flies to humans.

MATERIALS

- computer or tablet
- Homeobox Genes Diagram
- Homologous Structures Diagrams
- poster paper or construction paper (optional)

DIAGRAMS

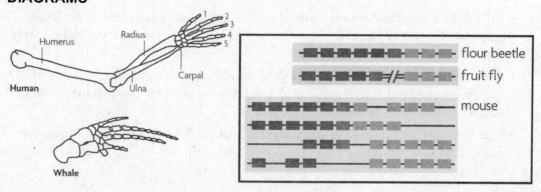

| B.5.2: Communicating Evidence of Evolution *continued*

MEET THE CHALLENGE

1. Create a table to record your observations about four lines of evidence for evolution and common ancestry. The lines of evidence that you will investigate are homologous structures, molecular and genetic evidence, embryology, and fossil evidence. Leave space in your table to write observations and conclusions about each type of evidence.

2. Observe the human arm and whale flipper bones. Write three similarities and three differences that you see in these structures.

3. Write your conclusions about how these homologous structures support the theory of evolution. How do these structures support the idea that populations have changed over time to adapt to their environment? How do these structures support the idea that these species share a common ancestor?

4. Observe the flour beetle, fruit fly, and mouse homeobox genes. Write three similarities and three differences that you see in these gene sequences.

5. Write your conclusions about how these gene sequences support the theory of evolution. Describe how sequences support the idea that these species have a common ancestor.

6. Use the Internet or the *Student Edition* to find information about two other lines of evidence of evolution: embryological evidence and fossil evidence. Record your observations and conclusions in your table, making sure to include any details relevant to change over time and common ancestry.

7. If time allows, research another line of evidence for evolution and include your findings in the table.

DOCUMENTATION

1. Use your observations and conclusions to prepare a presentation or pamphlet that communicates the lines of evidence for evolution. Your evidence should include evidence for change over time and for common ancestry.

2. **Format** Decide on a format for your presentation.

   • Think about who your audience will be. Which format would be the best way to communicate information about the lines of evidence you observed?

   • Think about the length of your presentation or pamphlet. How many minutes or pages should it be? How can you briefly explain the most important findings?

3. **Content** Decide which types of information should be included in your presentation.

   • Include information about each line of evidence. Discuss each piece of evidence and how it supports the theory of evolution, including the principles of change over time and common ancestry.

   • Give specific evidence that supports your conclusions. For example, give specific gene sequences and describe, in detail, how they support the idea that two or more species had a common ancestor.

   • Cite the sources of information in your presentation. Follow a standard format for citing scientific sources.

B.5.3: Microevolution and Antibiotic-Resistant Bacteria

B.5.2 Apply concepts of statistics and probability to support a claim that organisms with an advantageous heritable trait tend to increase in proportion to organisms lacking this trait.

Challenge Activity

Challenge: In this exercise you will work with a model bacterial population. You will examine how the population changes over time and in response to environmental pressures such as antibiotics.

The discovery and mass production of antibiotics is one of the greatest achievements of biotechnology. However, the widespread use of antibiotics has had an unintended consequence: the evolution of antibiotic-resistant bacteria, or bacteria that can no longer be killed by a specific antibiotic. If these bacteria infect a person, several different types of antibiotics may need to be tried—if the infection can be treated at all.

MATERIALS

- chips, colored (100)
- chips, white (100)
- number cubes (2)

Table 1. Model Key		
Sum of Number Cubes	**Event Description**	**Effect on Population**
4, 5, or 6	Nutrients are plentiful.	The population doubles.
10	Nutrients are low.	If there are fewer than 10 bacteria, the population is not affected. If there are more than 10, two-thirds of the population dies.
12	The bacteria come into contact with a cleaning product.	Ninety percent of the bacteria die.
11	Antibiotic A is put into the environment.	All nonresistant bacteria in the colony are killed.
3	One bacterium mutates so that it is resistant to antibiotic A.	One nonresistant bacterium (white) is replaced by an antibiotic-resistant bacterium (colored).
2	An antibiotic A–resistant bacterium in the population shares DNA with 10% of the other bacteria.	If there are antibiotic-resistant bacteria in your population, 10% of the nonresistant bacteria are converted to antibiotic-resistant bacteria.
7, 8, or 9	No change occurs in the environment.	No change occurs in the population.

MEET THE CHALLENGE

1. Count out 20 white chips. This group of chips represents a bacterial population; each chip is an individual bacterium. The white chips are the nonresistant bacteria—they are susceptible to being killed by antibiotic A. The colored chips represent antibiotic-resistant bacteria—those that are not killed by antibiotic A.

2. Roll the two number cubes and add the resulting numbers together. Look up the total in the Model Key in Table 1 and find the corresponding event description and effect on the population.

3. Figure out how you would change your population to reflect the event. For example, if a bacterium is "killed," you would remove it from your population. If one bacterium develops antibiotic resistance, you would exchange it for a colored chip. Always round the number of bacteria that are affected by an event to the nearest whole number. For example, if you have 20 bacteria in your population and two-thirds of them die, that would mean 13.3 die. You would then round the number to 13 and remove 13 chips from your population.

4. Draw Table 2 as shown. Include 20 rows for your data. Record your results.

Table 2. Population Changes Over Time				
Roll of Number Cubes	Number Cube Total	Event	Number of White Chips	Number of Colored Chips
1st				
2nd				

5. Continue to roll the number cubes and change your population accordingly. For each roll, fill in the rows in Table 2 describing the event and modifications to your population. Stop after 20 rolls. If your population is wiped out before 20 rolls, do the activity again. Keep track of your population as you did before.

6. Total the number of bacteria in your final population and determine what percentage is resistant to antibiotic A.

DOCUMENTATION

1. **Analyze** How did adding antibiotic A to the environment affect the population of bacteria? Was antibiotic resistance an advantageous trait in this environment? Why?

2. **Calculate** Imagine that all of the classroom's populations were grouped into one large population. What percentage of this population would have antibiotic-resistant bacteria?

3. **Infer** How might the population have been different if antibiotic A–resistant bacteria were not able to share DNA with other bacteria in the population?

4. **Conclude** Antibiotics are often found in the environment. For example, in the United States, antibiotics are used on livestock and poultry meant for human consumption. Write a statement explaining what effects this could have on bacterial populations in animals and humans and how natural selection is related to this change.

B.5.4: Evaluating Evidence of Patterns in Evolution

B.5.4 Evaluate evidence to explain the role of natural selection as an evolutionary mechanism that leads to the adaptation of species, and to support claims that changes in environmental conditions may result in: (1) increases in the number of individuals of some species, (2) the emergence of new species over time, and/or (3) the extinction of other species.

Challenge Activity

Challenge: Read and evaluate articles claiming that changes in the environment can lead to the emergence and extinction of species.

Evaluating evidence involves defending and critiquing claims and explanations about the natural world. You can evaluate evidence by assessing how well the evidence supports the claim and by determining whether the evidence is valid. To begin the process of evaluating sources, ask yourself these questions as you read each article:

• What is the source of the information? Is this a credible source?

• Is there enough evidence to support the claim that is being made?

• Is the evidence accurate or does it contain errors?

• Does the evidence match the claim that is being made?

MATERIALS

• computer, tablet, or personal device with Internet access

• *Student Edition* Unit 5 BioZine Article: Climate Change—Changing the Planet

• *Student Edition* Unit 7 BioZine Article: Genetically Modified Foods—Do Potential Problems Outweigh Benefits?

MEET THE CHALLENGE

1. Read the *Student Edition* Unit 5 BioZine Article: Climate Change—Changing the Planet. Answer Questions 1a, 1b, 3a, and 3b in the Questions section of this activity.

2. Read the *Student Edition* Unit 7 BioZine Article: Genetically Modified Foods—Do Potential Problems Outweigh Benefits? Answer Questions 2a, 3a, and 3b.

3. Use the Internet or another resource to find two additional articles related to either climate change or genetic engineering and their effects on species emergence and extinction. If your teacher approves, you may also search for articles related to other environmental factors that affect species, such as deforestation or drought.

4. Answer Questions 3a and 3b after reading each article.

5. Write an evaluation of the two articles you read, addressing every item in the Documentation section for each article.

QUESTIONS

1. **Climate Change—Changing the Planet**

   a. How might climate change cause the extinction of some species?

   b. How might climate change benefit some species?

2. **Genetically Modified Foods—Do Potential Problems Outweigh Benefits?**

   a. How might growing genetically modified crops cause the emergence of new species called "superweeds"?

3. **General Questions (answer for all articles)**

   a. What claim is made in the article? (What is the author trying to say?)

   b. What evidence does the author give to support the claim? (Are there data, statistics, patterns, or facts provided that support the claim?)

DOCUMENTATION

1. **Source Information** Explain what source you will be evaluating.

   • Give the title, author, publisher, and year the article was written.

   • Describe the origin of the source (newspaper, webpage, scientific journal).

2. **Claim** Describe the statements made in the article.

   • What claim is made in the article? (See answers to Question 3a.)

3. **Evaluating Evidence** Evaluate the evidence by addressing these points.

   • What evidence is given? (See answers to Question 3b.)

   • Is the evidence adequate? Is there enough evidence present to make the claim?

   • Is the evidence accurate? Does the evidence conflict with other evidence?

   • Is the evidence relevant? Does the evidence line up with the claim being made?

4. **Credibility** In your opinion, is this source credible and reliable?

B.5.5: Natural Selection

B.5.5 Construct an explanation based on evidence that the process of evolution primarily results from four factors: (1) the potential for a species to increase in number, (2) the heritable genetic variation of individuals in a species due to mutation and sexual reproduction, (3) competition for limited resources, and (4) the proliferation of those organisms that are better able to survive and reproduce in the environment.

Challenge Activity

Challenge: Use a simulation to make observations about a population of rabbits and explain how the observations are related to the principles of natural selection.

BACKGROUND

During his voyage on the HMS *Beagle*, Charles Darwin was struck by the variation of traits in species that he observed. For example, on the Galapagos Islands, Darwin observed finches with different types of beaks. Finches with strong, thick beaks lived in areas with a lot of large, hard-shelled nuts, while those species of finches with more delicate beaks were found where insects or fruits were widely available.

These observations led Darwin to develop his theory of natural selection. Natural selection is a mechanism by which individuals that have inherited beneficial adaptations produce more offspring on average than do other individuals. There are four main principles to the theory of natural selection.

- **Overproduction** While having many offspring raises the chance that some will survive, it also results in competition between offspring for resources.

- **Variation** The heritable differences, or variations, that exist in every population are the basis for natural selection. The differences among individuals result from differences in the genetic material of the organisms, whether inherited from a parent or resulting from a genetic mutation.

- **Competition** Sometimes a certain variation allows an individual a better chance of survival than other individuals it competes against in its environment. More successful individuals are "naturally selected" to live longer and to produce more offspring that share those adaptations for their environment.

- **Descent with modification** Over time, natural selection will result in species with adaptations that are well suited for survival and reproduction in an environment. More individuals will have the trait in every following generation, as long as the environmental conditions continue to remain beneficial for that trait.

MATERIALS

computer with Internet access

MEET THE CHALLENGE

1. Use a search engine to search for "PhET" and "natural selection."

2. Find and run the Natural Selection simulation from the University of Colorado.

3. Click Download or Run Now according to your teacher's directions.

4. Click Brown Fur under Add Mutation. Then click the Add a Friend button.

5. Let the simulation run for a few generations. Then click Wolves under Selection Factor.

6. Let the simulation run for a few more generations. Then record your observations about the coat color of the rabbits in the row of the data table titled Trial 1.

7. Continue to let the simulation run for a few minutes, and then record your observations about the population of rabbits in the row of the data table titled Trial 1.

8. Click Play Again.

9. Click Long Teeth under Add Mutation and then click the Add a Friend button.

10. Let the simulation run for a few generations and then click Food under Selection Factor.

11. Record your observations about tooth length in the population of rabbits in the row of the data table titled Trial 2.

12. Experiment by changing another variable in the simulation. Record your observations in the row of the data table titled Trial 3.

Trial	Mutation	Selection Factor	Environment	Observations
Trial 1				
Trial 2				
Trial 3				

DOCUMENTATION

1. **Trial 1 Observations** Explain how the observations you made in Trial 1 are related to these principles of natural selection:

   - Individuals with beneficial traits are able to survive and pass down traits to their offspring, so more individuals will have those traits in the following generation.

   - Overproduction, which is having many offspring, increases the chance that some offspring will survive.

2. **Trial 2 Observations** Explain how the observations you made in Trial 2 are related to these principles of natural selection:

   - Mutation and sexual reproduction lead to genetic variation within a species.

   - There is competition for an environment's limited supply of the resources that individuals need to survive and reproduce.

3. **Apply and Extend** Propose another scenario in which natural selection could occur. Explain what type of organism makes up your population, what variations of traits exist in this population, and how the four principles of natural selection would result in the evolution of this population.

B.5.6: Interpret Data on History of Life

B.5.6 Analyze and interpret data for patterns in the fossil record and molecular data that document the existence, diversity, extinction, and change of life forms throughout the history of life on Earth under the assumption that natural laws operate today as in the past.

Challenge Activity

Challenge: Create a chart or poster that provides evidence from fossil records to show how life forms have changed throughout the history of life on Earth.

Over time, organisms change due to variety of factors. Evidence of these types of changes can be seen by examining and comparing fossils within rocks of different ages. For example, rocks that are more than 1 billion years old may have fossils of single-celled organisms. When you move to rocks that are about 550 million years old, the presence of multicellular organisms becomes prevalent. At 500 million years ago, ancient fish without jawbones surface; and at 400 million years ago, fish with jaws are found. As the rocks become more and more recent, the fossils look increasingly like the animals we observe today. A chart can show evidence found in fossils in a brief and understandable way. You begin gathering information about the age of rocks and the types of fossils found within them. You will use online resources and those provided to you by your teacher to gather relevant information. This information can then be displayed as sketches, pictures, or timelines to show how life forms have changed during the evolutionary process throughout the history of life on Earth.

MATERIALS

- computer
- Internet access
- markers or colored pencils
- online sources:
  - http://www.bbc.co.uk/nature/history_of_the_earth
  - https://www.newscientist.com/article/dn17453-timeline-the-evolution-of-life/
- other teacher-approved sources
- paper, various sizes
- photocopies or photos of fossils (optional)

MEET THE CHALLENGE

1. Use the Internet to search for information about the fossils, the age of rocks, and Earth's geologic history. Make sure to use information from credible sources such as universities or government agencies. The web page addresses for these sources often end with .edu or .gov. If you are not sure a source is credible, ask your teacher.
2. As you search, record your sources.
3. Use the guidelines in the Documentation section to create your chart or poster.

PLANNING QUESTIONS

1. What are the oldest known fossils on Earth?

2. What is paleobiology?

3. Why are biologists interested in geologic timelines?

4. What is comparative anatomy?

5. Which organisms show clear fossil evidence of structural change over time?

6. What is the disadvantage of depending only on dating the rocks in which fossils are found for reconstructing an evolutionary timeline?

7. What is a timeline?

8. What is radiometric dating?

9. What is relative dating?

10. What role does DNA analysis play in determining how organisms have changed throughout Earth's history?

11. Which information can be easily displayed on a chart or poster?

DOCUMENTATION

1. Use the Planning section and these instructions to create a visual chart of fossils that shows how organisms have changed over time.

2. **Audience** Choose the audience.

   • Decide who the audience is for this chart or poster. The audience could include the public or other students.

3. **Format** Choose a format.

   • Decide which format you will use to present your information. For example, will this be in the form of a timeline with fossil descriptions, or include sketches and photos?

4. **Content** Include essential information.

   • Choose an approach: Show how organisms have generally changed over time, or choose examples of specific species that have changed throughout Earth's history.

   • Choose and identify a wide range of rocks from different times that contain fossils of different ages.

   • Include information on the Earth's five mass extinction events where applicable.

   • Indicate that Earth's history can be represented as a timescale on which large chunks of time are called *periods* and smaller ones *epochs*. Tracking related fossil species through some of this geologic timeline may be useful in determining how they evolved.

   • If dealing with specific species and how their structures evolved (e.g., evolution of whales), use sketches or pictures of fossil evidence along with the geologic timeline in which these fossils were found.